001
Plum blossom
Symbol of winter

002
Butterfly

003
Flower

004
Phoenix
Symbol of the Empress, beauty, peace,
prosperity, sun

005
Shou, coins, and bat
Symbol of long life, wealth,
and happiness

006
Flower

007
Boat

008
Lion playing with balls
Symbol of valor, power

009
Parrot

010
Sunrise

011
Butterfly

012
Bird

013
Dragons and pearl

014
Mandarin ducks

015
Hsi and butterfly
Symbol of joy

3

016
Pomegranite

017
Flower

018
Hen

019
A junk

4

020
Hydrangea flower

021
Pavilion

022
Phoenixes and flower

023
Goldfish

025
Phoenix and *Shou*
Symbol of goodness,
beauty, and long life

024
Bird and flower

026
Phoenix singing to
the rising sun

027
Dragon and pearl

028
Goldfish

029
A pink

030
Plum blossom and magpie

031
Chrysanthemum

032
Butterfly

033
Lion and balls

034
Magpie and barberry

035
Barberry

036
Flower

8

037
Butterfly

038
Magpie

039
Dragon and pearl

040
Sacred jewel
Symbol of beauty and purity

041
Symbol of
longevity and wealth

042
Bamboo

043
Butterfly

044
Flower

045
Eagle preying on a chicken

046
Flower

047
Cock preying on a centipede

048
Flower

049
Flower

050
Phoenix
Emblem of the Empress

051
Dragon
Emblem of the Emperor

052
Grapes

053
Butterfly

054
Chrysanthemum

055
Chrysanthemums

056
Bird

057
Two magpies

058
Ssu Chi An Lo
A wish for happiness
throughout the Four
Seasons

059
Boat

060
Flower

061
Flower

062
Dragonfly

063
Dragon and
tiger fighting

064
Chrysanthemum

065
Flower

066
Waterlily, bats, and coins
Symbol of purity, long life, and wealth

067
Crane

068
Three *Shou* characters
Symbol of long life

069
Flower

070
Dragon and phoenix

071
Citron

072
Goldfish

074
Flower

073
Flower

075
Two cranes

076
Shou, bats, and coins
Symbol of longevity and
prosperity

077
Sheep

078
Mandarin ducks

079
Toad and coins
Symbol of wealth

081
Five venimous things: tiger, snake, lizard, centipede, and spider

080
Flower

082
Flower

083
Ch'u Men Chien Ts'ai
Venture forth if you would find your fortune

084
Snake devouring a frog

085
Flower

086
Crane

088
Barberry

087
Shou, bat, and butterfly
Symbol of long life and joy

089
Cat

090
Flower

091
Goose

092
Flower

093
Flower

094
Phoenix

095
Flower

096
Crane

097
Plum blossom

098
Rabbit

21

099
Flower

100
Pheasant

101
Tiger

102
Falling flowers

103
Flower

104
Rabbit

105
Lark and chicken

106
Magpie

107
Flower

109
Horse

108
Pheasant

110
Flower

111
Flower

112
Flower

113
Birds kissing

114
Chrysanthemum

115
Plum blossom

116
Flower

117
Flower

118
Comorant

119
Bat

120
Phoenix

121
Dragon

122
Flower

123
Flower

124
Chrysanthemum

125
Wasp

126
Phoenix

127
Flower

128
Flower

129
Clouds

130
Landscape

131
Boat

132
Dragon

133
Shou and five bats
Symbol of age, wealth, health,
and virtue

134
Carp

135
Landscape

136
Landscape

137
Thrush and chicken

138
Dragon

139
Butterflies

140
Moon and stars

141
Landscape

142
Landscape

143
Dragonflies

144
Goldfish

145
Flower

146
Unicorn

147
Shrimp

148
Landscape

149
Flower

150
Landscape

151
Flower

152
Flower

153
Landscape

154
Landscape

155
Landscape

156
Flower

157
Flower

158
Horse

159
Landscape

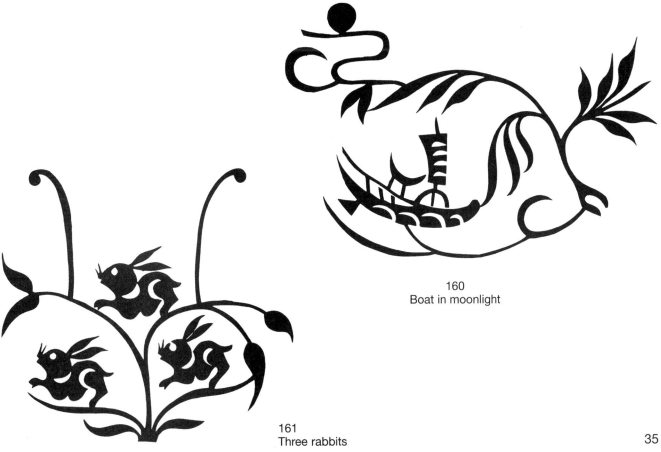

160
Boat in moonlight

161
Three rabbits

35

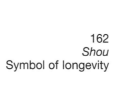
162
Shou
Symbol of longevity

163
Duck

164
Flower

165
Chiang T'ai-kung fishing in the
Wei River

166
Carp

167
Flower

168
Flower

169
Peach
Symbol of
immortality,
marriage, and
springtime

170
Barberry

171
Chinese persimmon

172
Flower

173
Lotus

174
Bamboo

175
Dragonfly

176
Carp leaping
through the
Dragon Gate

177
Flower

178
Flower

179
Unicorn

180
Citron and bat

181
Chrysanthemum

182
Mallow

183
Chrysanthemum

184
Flower

185
New moon

186
Flower

187
Flower

188
Flower

189
Dog and lotus

190
Flower

191
Flower

192
Chao Ts'ai Chin Pao
A charm to bring wealth

193
Fu Kuei Yu Yü
A charm to insure a
surplus of wealth

194
Huang Chin Wan Liang
A charm to bring 10,000 ounces of gold

195
Nien Nien Ju I
A charm to provide satisfaction
year by year

196
Huang Chin Wan Liang
A charm to bring 10,000
ounces of gold

197
Yang Yin and *Pa Kua* symbols

198
Shou and five bats
Symbol of longevity, wealth, and virtue

199
Monkey

200
Bird

201
Chu Ko-liang
A statesman of the
San Kuo period

202
Shou
Symbol of longevity

203
Ox

204
Goldfish

205
Carp

206
Kuan Yü
A famous general of the
San Kuo period

207
Mi Lo Fu - The Buddha Maitreya
Patron saint of goldsmiths and
silversmiths

208
Ch'ang Wo fleeing to
the moon

209
Squirrels

210
Flower

211
The *T'ang* Emperor *Ming* visits
the moon for pleasure

212
A fairy scattering
flowers

213
Yang Ssu-lang visits his
mother

215
Chung-li Ch'üan
Chief of the Eight Immortals

214
Tiger
Symbol of bravery

216
Unicorn carrying a boy child
A charm to insure male offspring

217
Ho Hsien-ku
One of the Eight Immortals

218
Han Hsiang-tzu
One of the Eight Immortals
Patron saint of musicians

219
Shou
Symbol of
longevity

220
Boy among flowers